Drama for Students, Volume 12

x

The Government Inspector

Nikolai Gogol

1836

Introduction

The Government Inspector, by Nikolai Gogol, has also been translated into English under the titles *The Inspector General,* and *The Inspector.* The written play was brought to the attention of the Tsar Nicholas I, who liked it so much that he insisted on its production. *The Government Inspector* premiered at the Alexandrinsky Theatre, in Saint

Petersburg, in 1836. The tsar, who was among the first to see the play, was said to have commented that the play ridiculed everyone—most of all himself.

The plot of *The Government Inspector* hinges on a case of mistaken identity, when a lowly impoverished young civil servant from Saint Petersburg, Hlestakov, is mistaken by the members of a small provincial town for a high-ranking government inspector. The town's governor, as well as the leading government officials, fear the consequences of a visit by a government inspector, should he observe the extent of their corruption. Hlestakov makes the most of this misconception, weaving elaborate tales of his life as a high-ranking government official and accepting generous bribes from the town officials. After insincerely proposing to the governor's daughter, Hlestakov flees before his true identity is discovered. The townspeople do not discover their mistake until after he is long gone and moments before the announcement of the arrival of the real government inspector.

The Government Inspector ridicules the extensive bureaucracy of the Russian government under the tsar as a thoroughly corrupt system. Universal themes of human corruption and the folly of self-deception are explored through this drama of Russian life. The governor's famous line, as he turns to address the audience directly, "What are *you* laughing at? You are laughing at yourselves," illustrates this theme, which is summed up in the play's epigraph, "If your face is crooked, don't literary figure, who provided him with ideas for two of his most important works.

In 1834, he began a position as assistant professor of medieval history at Saint Petersburg University. Gogol quickly proved himself a resounding failure as a professor, in part because he was not sufficiently knowledgeable in his subject, and left this post after only one year. During that year, Gogol, while generally neglecting his teaching duties, published two books of short stories, *Mirgorod* and *Arabesques;* a collection of essays; as well as two plays, *Marriage* and *The Government Inspector* (also translated variously as *The Inspector General,* and *The Inspector*). *The Government Inspector* was brought to the attention of the tsar, who liked it so much that he requested the first theatrical production, which was performed in 1836.

Gogol, reacting to heavy criticism by the government officials his play lampooned, declared that "everyone is against me" and left Russia. He spent the next twelve years in self-imposed exile. During this time, Gogol traveled extensively throughout Europe, staying in Germany, Switzerland, and Paris, eventually settling primarily in Rome. After Pushkin died in 1837, Gogol inherited the mantle of the leading Russian writer of the day. Gogol's literary masterpiece *Dead Souls* and the first edition of his collected works were published in 1842. In 1848, he returned to Russia, settling in Moscow.

Gogol became increasingly preoccupied with religious concerns, eventually taking council from a fanatical priest who influenced him to burn his manuscript for the second volume of *Dead Souls*. Gogol died at the age of forty-two in 1852 as the result of a religious fast.

Plot Summary

Act 1

The play is set in a small town in provincial Russia, in the 1830s. Act 1 takes place in a room in the governor's house. The governor has called together the town's leading officials—including the judge, the superintendent of schools, the director of charities, the town doctor, and a local police officer —to inform them that a government inspector is due to arrive from Saint Petersburg. The governor explains that this government inspector is to arrive "incognito" with "secret instructions" to assess the local government and administration of the town. The governor, in a panic, instructs his officials to quickly cover up the many unethical practices and general corruption of the local town authorities. The brothers Bobchinsky and Dobchinsky, two local landowners, rush in to inform the governor and his officials that they have seen the government inspector staying at the local inn. As the governor is leaving to greet the "Very Important Person" at the inn, his wife and his daughter, Marya, enter, asking about the inspector.

Act 2

Act 2 takes place in Hlestakov's room at the inn. Ossip, the middle-age servant of Hlestakov, muses that his master, a young man of about twenty-three years, is a government clerk of the lowest rank, who has lost all of his money gambling, and is unable to pay his bill for two weeks' food and lodging at the inn. The governor enters, assuming that Hlestakov is indeed the government inspector. He offers to show Hlestakov the local institutions, such as the prison, whereupon Hlestakov thinks he is being arrested for not paying his bill. The confusion continues, however, until the governor invites Hlestakov to stay at his home, and the young man goes along with this apparent generosity without understanding that he is being mistaken for someone else.

Act 3

Act 3 takes place in the governor's house. The governor's wife and daughter are eagerly awaiting the arrival of the government inspector. Hlestakov and the governor enter, the governor having given him a tour of the hospital and a hearty meal. Finally catching on that he is being mistaken for a high-ranking government official, Hlestakov launches into an elaborate fantasy of his luxurious and privileged life in Saint Petersburg. When Hlestakov retires to his room in the governor's house, the governor's wife and daughter bicker over which of them he was flirting with.

Act 4

Act 4 also takes place in the governor's house. The governor sends in each of his town officials to

Anna Andreyevna

Anna Andreyevna is the governor's wife. In his notes on the characters, Gogol describes her as "still tolerably young, and a provincial coquette," who "displays now and then a vain disposition." Her concern with appearance is indicated by the stage direction that "she changes her dress four times" during the play. The governor's wife flirts shamelessly with Hlestakov. When he informs her of his engagement to Marya, she approves, imagining the benefits she will enjoy in Saint Petersburg as a result of the marriage.

Bobchinsky

Bobchinsky, along with his brother Dobchinsky, is a landowner in the town. In his notes describing the characters, Gogol states that the brothers are "remarkably like each other." They are both "short, fat, and inquisitive. . . wear short waistcoats, and speak rapidly, with an excessive amount of gesticulation." Gogol distinguishes them by noting that "Dobchinsky is the taller and steadier, Bobchinsky the more free and easy, of the pair."

Dobchinsky

Dobchinsky, along with his brother Bobchinsky, is a landowner in the town. It is Bobchinsky and Dobchinsky who first see Hlestakov at the inn and mistake him for the government inspector. They immediately run to tell the governor that the government inspector has arrived, thus initiating the case of mistaken identity that propels the entire play.

The Governor

The governor of the town has the most to fear from the arrival of the government inspector because he has the most power of anyone in the town and is the most corrupt. In his notes on the characters, Gogol describes the governor as "a man who has grown old in the state service," who "wears an air of dignified respectability, but is by no means incorruptible." When Hlestakov announces that he has become engaged to the governor's daughter, the governor immediately indulges himself in fantasies of the luxurious, high status life he will enjoy in Saint Petersburg as a result.

Media Adaptations

- *The Government Inspector* was adapted to the screen in a 1949 American film entitled *The Inspector General*. It starred Danny Kaye as the character of Hlestakov and was directed by Henry Foster.

Hlestakov

Hlestakov, also spelled Khlestakov, is a young man of about twenty-three. He is a government clerk of the lowest rank and is traveling through the small town accompanied by his servant, Ossip. Hlestakov has lost all of his money gambling and is unable to pay his food and lodging bill at the inn. The people of the town mistake him for the government inspector, who was set to arrive there incognito to check up on the workings of the local government. Hlestakov at first thinks the governor intends to arrest and imprison him for not paying his bill but eventually realizes that he is being treated as an honored guest of the town. Hlestakov makes the most of this opportunity, weaving elaborate lies about his life in Saint Petersburg, gorging himself at a feast they have provided, milking the local government officials for all of the bribery money he can, and offering a false proposal of marriage to the governor's daughter. Hlestakov leaves town just before a letter posted to his friend and revealing his chicanery is intercepted and read by the town's postmaster—who brings it before the governor. By this time, Hlestakov is far gone; he is out of reach of any revenge that the townspeople may have wished to exact upon him. Gogol insisted that the character of Hlestakov is not calculatingly deceitful but an opportunist, merely making the most of the case of mistaken identity into which he has fallen.

Marya

Marya is the governor's daughter. She and her mother rush to the inn to meet the reputed government inspector. She responds to Hlestakov's flirtations and accepts his marriage proposal. Hlestakov, however, flees the town, telling her that he will return in several days to get her, but he has no intention whatsoever of doing so or of following up on his proposal.

during Gogol's lifetime?

- Gogol is from a region of Russia that is now the independent nation of the Ukraine. Learn more about the history and culture of the Ukraine in the nineteenth century. Learn more about the Ukraine today. How has the region changed since Gogol's youth?

- In addition to Gogol, important nineteenth century Russian writers include Aleksandr Pushkin, Fyodor Dostoyevsky, Leo Tolstoy, and Anton Chekhov. Learn more about one of these authors. When and where did he live and write? What are his most important literary works? What similarities, if any, can be found between his work and Gogol's?

- The Moscow Art Theater, established in 1895, was a center for innovative techniques in acting and dramatic production in Russia. Learn more about the history of the Moscow Art Theater. What influence do you think these innovative techniques had on productions of Gogol's plays?

from all the women as though from one bosom." Gogol insisted that "Disregard of these instructions may ruin the whole effect." Victor Erlich comments in his book *Gogol* that this tableau vivant is a "moment of truth," in which, "The lightning which strikes dumb the cast. . . illuminates, in retrospect, the real nature and drift of the proceedings." Richard Peace notes that, in this final moment, "the characters await their fate like the motionless figures of a run-down clock, whose time has suddenly runout."

Censorship

Under the reign of Tsar Nicholas I, Russian writers suffered extremely strict censorship of all written material. In 1826, a statute on censorship, according to Beresford,"prohibited the publication of any matter that was deemed to disparage the monarchy or the church or which criticized, even indirectly, the existing order of society." The years 1848-1855, particularly, were referred to as "the age of terror by censorship." Brown describes the crushing power of these censorship practices on Russian society: "Penalties included warnings, rebukes, fines, confiscations of offending books or magazines, police supervision or detention in the guardroom of local military garrisons." Brown concludes that "It was a wonder that anything got into print at all." Braun states that "Genuine Russian masterpieces" of dramatic writing "were suppressed by a pathologically suspicious censor and were destined to wait over thirty years for their first public performances." Literary historians agree that, had it not been brought to the special attention of the tsar himself, who whimsically approved it, *The Government Inspector* would certainly have been censored from any theatrical production until many years later.

Compare & Contrast

- **1825-1855:** The reign of Tsar Nicholas I (1796-1855) as Emperor of Russia is characterized by extreme repression and extensive censorship of all printed materials.

  1917-1991: The Russian Revolution of 1917 results in the end of the era of imperial Russia and the formation of the Union of Soviet Socialist Republics (U.S.S.R.)

  1985-1991: The ascendance of Mikhail Gorbachev as president of the U.S.S.R. results in the policies of *Glasnost* (verbal openness) and *Perestroika* (policy of economic and governmental reform), which usher in an era of unprecedented openness as well as the relaxation of censorship and repressive measures. These measures lead to the dissolution of the U.S.S.R. in 1991.

- **1712-1917:** St. Petersburg, located about four hundred miles northwest of Moscow, and founded by order of the Tsar Peter I the Great in 1703, is made the new capital of Russia in 1912. In the eighteenth century, St. Petersburg becomes a center of intellect and the arts. The population of St. Petersburg increases from over

Russian language and one of the acknowledged masterpieces of world drama."

Because of extremely strict censorship under the reign of the Tsar Nicholas I, Gogol's play might not have been produced in his lifetime. However, the poet Zhukovsky brought the written play directly to the attention of the tsar, who liked it so much that he insisted on a production at the royal theater. *The Government Inspector* opened in 1836, with the tsar in attendance. Nicholas was said to have delighted in the production.

Popular and critical reception of the play, however, has been dubbed by several critics a "succes de scandale"—meaning that the play's popular success was inextricable from its controversial critical reception. While the tsar himself was not offended by the play's open satire of the Russian bureaucracy, the audience members, most of whom were themselves civil servants, took personal offense. Nigel Brown notes that, "it is virtually the first work of art to expose to ridicule aspects of the administrative and bureaucratic system of Tsarist Russia." As a result, Erlich observes, "The story of the reception of *The Inspector General* and of Gogol's subsequent reaction is almost as interesting as the play itself." He explains:

> The initial impact was explosive. While the audiences' responses were mixed, hardly anyone remained indifferent. The bulk of the theater going public, especially the officials

and the sycophants of the bureaucratic establishment, were displeased, indeed often scandalized, by the 'vulgarity' and 'coarseness' of the play, and by its slanderous, not to say subversive tenor.

Janko Lavrin explains that "The spectators enjoyed the piece, but they were cross with the author. For everyone saw himself personally insulted." Yet, "In spite of all the attacks on Gogol . . . the theatre was always crowded. For even those who disliked it could not help enjoying it." Erlich notes, "The play was making an impact; it was the talk of the town, the focus of a lively and loud controversy," thus making Gogol,"one of the best-known and most talked-about writers of his time."

Taken aback by the extensive negative reaction to the play, Lindstrom notes that Gogol wrote to a friend, "Everyone is against me." In self-defense, he published an article,"After the Theater," which recounted the overheard dialogue of theatregoers leaving at the end of the play. *After the Theater* was later expanded and published in book form in 1842. Lindstrom comments that,"Of little artistic merit, it is nevertheless a valuable record of Gogol's increasing insistence on the didactic role of literature and his need to explain his art in terms of moral and social philosophy." Gogol, however, was so traumatized by the controversy raised by *The Government Inspector* that he quickly left the country, remaining in self-imposed exile for the next twelve years. He revised the play extensively,

Sources

Adams, Amy Singleton. *Dictionary of Literary Biography, Volume 198: Russian Literature in the Age of Pushkin and Gogol: Prose,* edited by Cristine A. Rydel, The Gale Group, 1999, pp. 137-166.

Beresford, M., "Introduction," in *The Government Inspector: A Comedy in Five Acts,* by N. V. Gogol, Edwin Mellen Press, 1996, pp. V, 1-94.

Braun, Edward, "Introduction," in *Nikolai Gogol: The Government Inspector,* edited by Edward O. Marsh and Jeremy Brooks, Methuen & Co., 1968, pp. 7-14.

Brown, Nigel, *Notes on Nikolai Gogol's The Government Inspector,* Heinemann, 1974, pp. 2, 4, 30, 36.

Campbell, D. J., "Forward," in *The Government Inspector,* by Nikolai Gogol, Heinemann, 1947, pp. 15-22.

Erlich, Victor, *Gogol,* Yale University Press, 1969, pp. 100-101, 103, 105-109.

Lavrin, Janko, *Gogol,* Routledge, 1926, 13-15, 153-154, 156.

-----, "Introduction," in *The Government Inspector,* by Nikolai Gogol, Heinemann, 1947, pp. 8-14.

Lindstrom, Thais S., *Nikolay Gogol,* Twayne, 1974, pp. 1-7, 115-116, 119-121.

Peace, Richard, *The Enigma of Gogol,* Cambridge University Press, 1981, pp. 1, 181.

Lightning Source UK Ltd.
Milton Keynes UK
UKHW010701071022
410089UK00014B/779